A New True Book

ANIMAL HOMES

By Illa Podendorf

*This "true book" was prepared
under the direction of
Illa Podendorf,
formerly with the Laboratory School,
University of Chicago*

CHILDRENS PRESS, CHICAGO

Bats sleep and hibernate
in caves.

PHOTO CREDITS

Jerry Hennen—Cover, 2, 6, 9 (right), 10, 12
(2 photos), 17, 18 (bottom), 19, 22 (left and bottom),
29 (left), 35, (top), 40 (top, left and right), 43 (2
photos), 44 (bottom)

Lynn M. Stone—4, 8 (2 photos), 9 (left), 11, 15, 18
(top), 25, 26, 28 (top right), 30 (2 photos), 34 (bottom),
42, 45 (left)

Allan Roberts—7, 14, 16 (left), 27, 32, 33 (top), 40
(bottom)

Reinhard Brucker—16 (right)

Len Meents—19 (drawing)

Root Resources—© Ted Farrington, 21

James P. Rowan—29 (right), 33 (bottom), 34 (top), 35
(bottom), 36 (2 photos), 38, 45 (right)

USDA (United States Department of Agriculture)—37

Mark Rosenthal—39

Louise T. Lunak—44 (top)

Cover: Prairie Dog

Library of Congress Cataloging in Publication Data

Podendorf, Illa.
    Animal homes.

    (A New true book)
    Rev. ed. of: The true book of animal homes.
    ©1960.
    Includes index.
    Summary: Describes a variety of animal homes,
shelters constructed by man for domesticated and zoo
animals, and explains that some animals do not build
homes.
    1. Animals, Habitations of—Juvenile
literature. [1. Animals—Habitations]
I. Title.
QL756.P6 1982   591.56′4   82-4466
ISBN 0-516-01666-0   AACR2

TABLE OF CONTENTS

Baby cottontail rabbit

SOME ANIMAL HOMES
ARE ON TOP
OF THE GROUND

Many animals make their homes on top of the ground.

Cottontail rabbits make nests in fields in the spring.

Baby cottontail rabbits in their nest

A cottontail's nest is warm. It is made from soft grass and lined with fur. The mother lines the nest with fur from her own body.

In winter, cottontails do not live in nests. Then they live under a barn or under some corn stalks.

Sometimes white-footed mice make their nests among plants on top of the ground.

White-footed mouse

Red fox cub (left) and its den (above)

A fox does not do much
building to make its home.
It finds a hollow log or a
hole among the rocks and
makes its den there.

SOME ANIMAL HOMES
ARE ABOVE THE GROUND

Sometimes squirrels make nests of twigs and sticks in branches of trees. Other times squirrels make homes in holes in trees. These homes are usually their winter homes.

Eastern gray squirrel and its nest

Raccoon nest

Raccoons live near water in woods. Some raccoons make their homes in hollow trees.

Garden
spider and
its web

A garden spider lives
among plants. A garden
spider spins a web. It
stays on or near its web.

Wooden beehives (above) and a bee nest in a hollow tree (right)

A honeybee lives with many other honeybees. Sometimes they make their homes in hollow trees.

Other times they make their homes in boxes that people make. A honeybee home is called a hive.

Bees fill their homes
with honeycomb. They
make honeycomb out of
wax. Each little honeycomb
room has six sides.

The little rooms are
called cells.

The honeybees store
food in some of the cells.
The food is honey. Queen
bees lay their eggs in
some of the cells.

Bees do many things.

Worker bees and the larger drones in a beehive.
You can see the six-sided cells.

Some bees help keep
the hive safe.
Other bees keep the
hive clean.
Many animals make
homes above the ground.

SOME ANIMAL HOMES ARE IN THE GROUND

Ground squirrels build homes under the ground. Their home is a long hall. This hall is called a tunnel. Sometimes the ground squirrels leave a pile of dirt at the door to their home.

Golden mantled ground squirrel

Badger at the opening of its den (above) and a groundhog burrow (right)

Prairie dogs, chipmunks, groundhogs, and badgers live underground, too. If you look for them, it is easy to see where they dig their tunnels.

Skunk
nesl

Skunks often make their homes in holes in the ground. They sometimes dig new holes. But they may use a hole that some other animal has made. Sometimes skunks crawl under buildings and make their homes there.

Black-tailed prairie dogs (above) and eastern chipmunks (right) live underground.

Many animals make their homes in holes in the ground.

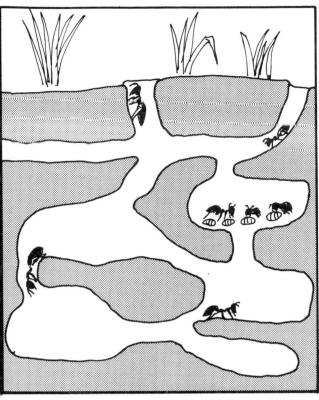

DIAGRAM OF ANT TUNNELS

Ant hill

Some kinds of ants build
their homes underground.
They dig a hole under a
rock or log. They dig on
and on until they have a
long tunnel underground.

19

Ants make more than one tunnel. At the end of each tunnel they make a room. In an ant home there are many tunnels and many rooms.

The first room to be made is a nursery. The baby ants live here.

Many of the rooms are storerooms for food. The worker ants bring back food to put in the storerooms.

SOME ANIMAL HOMES
ARE IN WATER

Beavers build their homes in water.

Sometimes they do not find a pond in which to make their homes. Then they must make a pond. They make a pond by building a dam.

Beaver dam

Beavers build their dams
out of mud, twigs,
branches, small logs, and
stones. They cut down
trees with their teeth.

They build the dam across a creek. The dam stops the water from running down the creek. The water spreads out and makes a big lake or pond.

Many beaver families may live together in one pond. Each year they work together to make their home safe and strong.

Beaver families live in the same pond year after year. Each fall they fix the holes in the dams and make the dams strong again.

They pile a lot of food near their homes. Their winter food is twigs and bark from pieces of wood.

Beaver lodge

A beaver's home has a
big room above water. The
door to the home is
underwater. A beaver
swims underwater and up
into the room of his home.

Muskrat lodge

Many animals make homes in water.

Some kinds of fish build nests.

A stickleback builds a nest of waterweeds. The mother fish lays eggs in the nest. Then the father fish protects them from the enemies.

Male longear sunfish

Sunfish make a nest at
the bottom of a pond. The
father brushes a place
clean with his fins. Then
the mother fish lays her
eggs. They both protect
the nest from their enemies.

Elk (above), pronghorn
(above right), moose (right)

SOME ANIMALS
NEVER BUILD HOMES

These animals move
about. Wherever they are
is their home.

Green frog (left), and painted
turtles in a farm pond (above)

Frogs live in ponds.
Some turtles live in
ponds, too.

Toad

Garter snake

Toads live in our gardens.

Garter snakes live in yards and hide among rocks and plants.

These animals' homes are any place they happen to be.

PEOPLE BUILD HOMES FOR ANIMALS

Many people build
homes for their pets.
Dogs may live in a
doghouse.

St. Bernard
with her
puppies

Siamese kittens

Kittens may sleep in baskets.

Birds live in cages.

Parakeet

Goldfish

Fish live in bowls.
Hamsters and gerbils
live in cages.

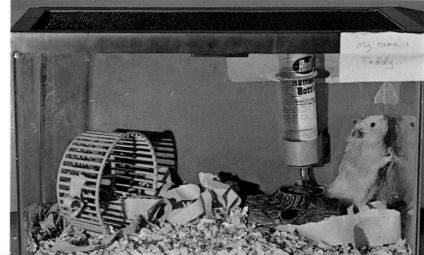

Angora
hamster

Rabbit
hutch

Pet rabbits may have a
home like this.
Farmers build homes for
their animals.
Cows live in a barn.

Cow barn

Horses live in a barn, too.
Pigs live in a house like
this.

Chickens live in a house
like this.

Sheep may live in a
house.

Lions in a zoo

Zookeepers always build
homes for their animals.

Black capped chickadee nest

Porcupine in ponderosa
pine tree

Woodchuck in
its burrow

40

THINGS TO REMEMBER

Animals live in many places.

Some animals live in the ground.

Some animals live high above the ground.

Alligator and turtles

Some animals live in water.

Mountain goat

Other animals live on land.

Elk

Horned toad

Deer

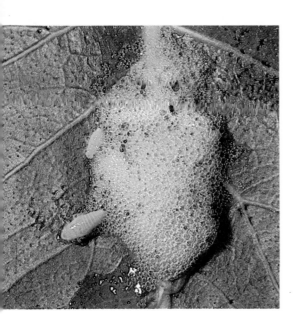

Spittlebug home (left) and bald-faced
hornet nest (above)

Some animals live in the
woods. Others live on the
desert.

Some kinds of animals
build unusual homes.

Each animal home is
just right for the animal
that builds and lives in it.

WORDS YOU SHOULD KNOW

cell(SELL) — a small part of a honeybee's hive.

dam — a wall built across a river or other body of water.

den — a home of a wild animal.

desert(DEZ • ert) — a dry region usually covered with sand.

enemy(EN • ih • mee) — not a friend.

fin — a thin, flat part that sticks out from the body of a fish or other water animal.

hive — the home for bees.

hollow(HAHL • oh) — to have an empty space or hole inside.

honeycomb(HUN • ee • coam) — a wax container made by honeybees to hold honey.

nursery(NER • ser • ee) — a place where young plants or animals are raised.

protect(pro • TEKT) — to keep safe; free from harm.

stalk(STAWK) — the main stem of a plant.

stickleback(STIK • ihl • back) — a kind of small fish.

tunnel(TUN • il) — a long hall under the ground that some animals dig.

unusual(un • YOO • zjoo • el) — not usual or common; different.

INDEX

About the Author

Born and raised in western Iowa, Illa Podendorf has had experience teaching science at both elementary and high school levels. For many years she served as head of the Science Department, Laboratory School, University of Chicago and is currently consultant on the series of True Books and author of many of them. A pioneer in creative teaching, she has been especially successful in working with the gifted child.